VIETNAMESE INSTANT POT COOKBOOK:

Popular Vietnamese recipes for Pressure Cooker. Quick and Easy Vietnamese Meals for Any Taste!

Henry Wilson

CONTENTS

INTRODUCTION

AN INSIGHT INTO VIETNAMESE CUISINE:

Vietnamese cuisine is very rich in aromas and taste and every dish has its own sternly desirable appeal. Despite the fact that the landscape of the country is very versatile, the Vietnamese cuisine is rich in lemongrass, cilantro, simmered beef bones, mint and the most important, the fish sauces. The food always has a balanced proportion of sweetness, fish-sauciness, aromatics, sourness, and heat. The basic theme of the cuisine is based on the 'yin and yang' principles, i.e. warm and cool, salty and sweet, and fermented and fresh. In the coming portions, we are going to describe this in detail.

The Vietnamese cuisine is very healthy and is solely based on fresh ingredients and a lesser amount of added butter, fats and oils. All the spices and herbs are carefully picked for adding a particular flavor to the dishes. All the herbs and spices are keenly combined with precision to have a particular balanced taste in the dishes. There are various fast food restaurants in the country but they aren't that crowded. You are going to find people having their meals together with their families and prefer a balanced meal instead of going out for fast food.

Just like the Chinese cuisine, the Vietnamese cuisine is based on the five flavor elements; i.e. bitter, sweet, salty, sour, and spicy. The cooking methods and techniques have been passed from generations to generations and the present day Vietnamese chefs are highly expert in making the best of the Vietnamese traditional dishes.

Geographical Importance:

The Vietnamese cuisine can be better understood by looking at the geographical position of the country. Vietnam is a very small, skinny country just like Italy, and having an S-shaped map. The country has China to its north, Cambodia, and Laos to the western side, and the South China Sea as its eastern border. The coastline of the country is approximately 3,000 km long and is stretched towards the downside, with Hanoi in the northern part. Saigon (also known as Hoi Chi Minh City) with rugged central highlands is located in the southern part. "The rice bowl of the country" also known as the fertile delta of Mekong is located in the bottom-most part.

The cuisines of the northern part are highly influenced by the Chinese cuisines with noodle- oriented soups and stir-fries. If you start your journey down, the cuisine gets more influence from neighboring Thailand and Cambodia, adding more flavors and taste. The southern part of the country has a tropical climate and is rich in jackfruit trees, abundant rice paddies, herb gardens, and coconut groves. The cuisines of southern Vietnam are generally sweeter, i.e., having an extra amount of palm sugar in savory dishes, the pho has generally sweeter broths, and the highly demanded coconut candies which are taffy-like, are prepared with coconut cream.

French Impact:

You cannot take out the French factor if you are considering the Vietnamese cuisine. The French colonization of Vietnam started in the Eighteenth century by the arrival of missionaries and lasted till around the initial years of the 1950s, i.e., 1954. The colonization had a strong influence on the lifestyle, cuisines, architecture, flavors, and land of the locals. The most prominent one is the banh mi, which has a highly crusty French baguette as its foundation. The Vietnamese have taken a step above this sandwich and added their own taste to it by adding fish patties, cilantro, grilled pork, sardines, chili-spiked carrots, and various other fillings.

Another remarkable impact of the French colonization on the Vietnamese cuisine is the pho (it is pronounced as 'fuh', the 'ph' giving an 'f' sound). The pho is basically comprised of French-minded meat broths and blended with Vietnamese rice noodles. A theory proposes that the word 'pho' is the phonetic imitation of the word 'feu' which is used for 'fire' in the French language like 'pot-au-feu'. Various people ponder that the French colonizers had slaughtered a huge chunk of animals to satisfy their tastes for steaks. The Vietnamese cooks were highly resourceful and would utilize the bones, ascraps, and the rest of the rejected parts to prepare pho.

Broths play a pivotal role in the Vietnamese cuisine and have critical importance in courtship. The mothers chose the wives of their sons on the basis of the wife's expertise in the preparation of broth' Preparing a lackluster broth is going to discard your chances of getting married to a guy! The experts in broth could state the exact stage of the broth by merely sniffing it. In conclusion, the Vietnamese are very strict and serious about their broths.

Basic Ingredients:

The basic or the building ingredients of almost every dish in Vietnam is fish and rice sauce. Wherever you travel in Vietnam, almost every food is themed on fish and rice sauces.

After Thailand, Vietnam is the second largest rice exporting nation in the world. Rice has grown abundantly in almost every part of the country. But, the fertile Mekong Delta located in the southern part of the country is the best rice producing area i.e. capable of producing enough rice for the entire population of Vietnam which is about 87 million people. That is not the end, despite feeding the entire country, the Delta produces a large quantity of rice which allows it to be further exported to various countries.

You can easily see that rice is a part of every meal, irrespective of its time, be it breakfast, lunch, dinner or even desserts. Of course, there is the presence of rice noodles, sticky rice, puffed rice snacks, rice paper wrappers, rice wine, fried rice, rice porridge, and regular ol' rice. It is almost hard to stay away from rice for a few hours while you are in Vietnam.

Rice is so culturally involved with them that they even say 'cơm muối' i.e. 'rice and salt', instead of gesundheit in response to sneezing. For instance, it means that if you want to bless someone or wish them better health, simply say rice and salt and that is going to fade away all the disease they are having.

The salt consumption in the entire Vietnamese cuisine usually comes from the fish sauce. A fermented, funky, and salty fish sauce which is also called nước mắm in the Vietnamese language is abundantly used in salad dressings, marinades, spring roll dips, broths, and almost every other dish you can possibly point out in the Vietnamese cuisine. Fish sauce is so important that the national condiment which is called the 'nước chấm' in the Vietnamese language is prepared from fish sauce which is slightly diluted with a mere splash of garlic, sugar, lime juice, and chilies.

The best, and high-quality fish sauce is made in Phu Quoc, which is basically an island closely located near the Cambodian border. The water surrounding Phu Quoc has   an abundant amount of plankton and seaweed, which keeps the abundant population of anchovy very happy. You can make fish sauce from any fish, but the best fish sauce is made from anchovies that are harvested near the Phu Quoc Island. The Vietnamese love their fish sauce as much as the Americans love cheese.

The fish sauce is produced in various factories where salt and tiny fishes are aged for around 6 months in wooden barrels. These fish sauces are the best in the country and are high in demand due to their presence in almost every food in Vietnamese cuisine.

Aromatics and Herbs:

There is a geographical history associated with the herbs and spices used in Vietnamese cuisine. Vietnam had been usually isolated and wasn't a great partner in the spice trading. As a general rule, anything that is produced in Vietnam is going to be a good point to ponder about what would be the best spot for it in the cuisine. Ingredients like chili powders and chilies were added later on in the Vietnamese cuisine when spice traders expanded their business to include Vietnam. The Vietnamese foods are comprised of an abundant amount of aromatics, spices, and herbs. They can either be in the steamy pots of pho or enclosed with a pancake called Banh xeo or even wrapped into spring rolls.

All the ingredients in the Vietnamese cuisine are very fresh. Almost every food of the Vietnamese contain herbs, spices, and various other aromatics and the best dish is served only when all the ingredients are highly fresh.

Some of the important herbs, aromatics, and chilies used in the Vietnamese cuisine are as follows:

1. **Mint:**
   There are various verities of mint that are produced in Vietnam. They include fuzzy, lemony tasted, spicy tasted, etc.
2. **Cilantro:**
   It is used in various spring rolls, soups, salads, and various other dishes. They are also used abundantly in garnishing. It depends on your genetics if the cilantro tastes soapy or not.
3. **Lime Leaf:**

   It is shiny and bright green in appearance and is used in some oils that are bitter.

4. **Basil:**
   Although it is generally more popular in Thailand, in the Vietnamese cuisine, it is used on herb plates and in pho.

5. **Fish leaf or fish mint:**
   Clear from the name, this herb is having a certain pungent smell and taste like fishes. It tastes exactly like a fish.
6. **Garlic Chives:**
   They have onion and garlic flavor and are flat leaves.
7. **Scallions and green onions.**
8. **Lemongrass:**
   As from the name, they smell and tastes like lemon. They are used in both savory and sweet dishes.
9. **Turmeric:**
   They are also knowns as poor man's saffron. They add a peppery flavor and certain vivid godliness to various fried foods.
10. **Dill:**
    They are not that popular in other South Asian cuisines but they are certainly used in the Vietnamese cuisine in a fish dish known as Cha Ca. this herb is treated as a vegetable instead of an herb in this dish.
11. **Saigon Cinnamon:**
    They are various varieties of cinnamon in the world but this one is particularly associated with Vietnamese cuisine. They are having a certain earthy, woody aroma and flavor and is mostly used in pho.
12. **Galangal and ginger:**
    They are both knobby rhizomes and are pervasive in the Vietnamese cuisine.
13. **Tamarind Pulp:**
    Although, this isn't used that much in the Vietnamese cuisine, yet this sweet-sour pulp is an ingredient in making curries and soups.
14. **Annatto Seeds:**
    They are used in foods to provide a specific lemony flavor and for coloring foods.
15. **Chili Powder:**

It is used not only for color but also for having a spicy flavor. Chili powder is more famous and used in the southern parts of the country as the northern parts still rely on black pepper as the major spice.

16. **Star anise:**

They are usually used in stews and soups to add a certain licorice flavor. They also are an important ingredient in various meat dishes too.

17. **Coconut Sugar:**

It is very popular in southern parts of the country for making soups but is not used abundantly as rock sugar. Rock sugar is very famous in the country and is used as a sweetener in desserts and drinks. It is also used in various savory dishes.

18. **Salt:**

Although it is used sparingly yet, it is a key ingredient in Vietnamese cuisine. There are very limited dishes which have no salt in them. Irrespective of this, the Vietnamese cuisine is considered to be healthier than the American cuisine due to the limited amount of salt used.

19. **Black pepper:**

The usage of black pepper is almost the same as its usage in American cuisine. It is widely used in stews and soups as well as in various meat dishes. Black pepper was the only spice used in Vietnamese cuisine before the introduction of chili powder. It hasn't lost its importance despite the introduction of fruits to the cuisine and the Vietnamese love their peppercorns even now.

Seasoning Blends:

Seasoning blends are not that much used in the Vietnamese cuisine as single spices. Generally, food is flavored with a small amount of one or two spices and a lot of herbs. As in Indian cuisine where spice blends are pretty common, the Vietnamese cuisine doesn't involve spice blends generally. There is a 'Vietnamese

Pork Rub' available in the market which is a spice blend based on the Vietnamese cuisine. It is created by Vietnamese chefs who have mastered the art of cooking various pork dishes. Pork is a very important part of the cuisine and this spice blend contains the exotic flavors of the Vietnamese cuisine. This blend can be used for seasoning grilled pork chops and pork tenderloin. It can also be used as an ingredient in pork gravies too.

Sauces:

Sauces are the most crucial part of the Vietnamese cuisine and it is incomplete without them. The Vietnamese cuisine is actually based on these sauces having a salty taste for providing a base touch but many dishes also include these sauces as a finishing touch.

1. The most abundantly used sauce is the **fish sauce** which is like a thick condiment. It is used in pho or even or grilled pork dishes apart from being the base for various stews and soups.

2. **Soy sauce** is also used in Vietnamese cuisine. It is generally used in veggies and has an umami flavor with a salty taste.

3. **Shrimp sauce** is used for marinating and sautéing meats and is actually a paste of salt and shrimp.

4. **Chili sauce** is also used abundantly in the Vietnamese cuisine. It gives out a reddish color to various light veggie broths or soups, apart from giving out a nice kick.

Vietnamese cuisine has evolved a bit and contains a small amount of MSGs, contrary to the common prejudice. "Gia vi" or "Bot canh" which is a mixture of pepper, salt and a little number of MSGs are used in the Vietnamese cooking widely I and in particular, the northern part of the country. The most popular spice choice for the Vietnamese cooks is poultry powder, sugar, pepper, gia yi, pepper and salt and a smaller dose of MSGs.

All the spies mentioned above are used in the Vietnamese cuisine but their usage may vary from place to place depending upon the landscape. As said earlier, black pepper is still used as the main spice in the northern parts of the country while the southern part uses chili powder. Importantly, the northern Vietnamese like their food saltier and less sweet than the rest of the country.

Central Vietnamese like their food savor, spicy and colorful. They prefer cooking with dried chilies instead of fresh ones for adding an extra spicy taste to their foods. Cooking methods in the southern part of the country are strongly influenced by Chinese, Thai and Cambodian cuisines. So, southern Vietnamese like their food spicy by adding more red chilies, and sweet by adding coconut milk or sugar in their foods.

Dairy:

There is no concept of fresh dairy but the cuisine includes an abundant quantity of sweetened condensed milk. There is a specific egg coffee available in Hanoi which is made by whipping a raw egg on the topmost layer of condensed and sweetened milk

It's important to note that there isn't any impact of Camembert or Brie by the French colonists. Clearly, there isn't any high usage of cheese, cream, or butter in the Vietnamese cuisine but the calcium intake is compensated by consuming fish shells and bones. Normally, you don't have to remove the tail of the shrimp, eat it completely so it will give you a crunchy taste.

In the case of fresh milk, you can easily spot lots of cans of sweetened condensed milk which is mostly used in the 'white coffee'. The sweet and thick layer of the milk is blended with locally grown dark roast coffee. This coffee is separately brewed via a metal drip filter for servings into various cups. In general, the amount of milk is higher than the amount of coffee in the cups.

Although the coffee is amazing and sweeter in taste, it is very strong.

Fruits:

Fruits are used both as veggies and in desserts in the Vietnamese cuisine. In general, unripe fruits are used as a veggie. For example, a green banana flower or papaya is used as the base of various salads instead of leafy greens. These fruits are usually ripe in taste and are blended with chili, dried shrimp, fish sauce, chopped peanuts, and garlic.

For ripe fruits, according to their wondrous and sweet taste, they are used for desserts. Generally, meals are followed by a large platter of fruits and a teapot instead of cookies or cakes. These include slices of mango, banana, watermelon, pineapple, papaya, lychees, and rambutans.

The unjust thing done to the Vietnamese cuisine available in the United States is that it is reduced merely to stir fry and rice because the cuisine has such rich-flavored and aromatic foods to offer other than rice and stir fry. In comparison with other various cuisines which are a part of the culture of the US, Vietnamese cuisine also has a a small standing in it.

Chicken Recipes

Caramelized Chicken

Servings: 8

Prep Time: 40 minutes

Ingredients:

For Marinade:

- 4 tablespoons fish sauce
- 3 red chilies, minced
- 4 tablespoons fresh ginger, minced finely
- 4 teaspoons garlic, minced finely
- 2 tablespoons sugar
- 8 (5-ounce) chicken thighs

For Sauce:

- 2 tablespoons canola oil
- 1/3 cup sugar
- 1 cup chicken broth
- 1 small yellow onion, sliced into petals

For Garnishing:

- ¼ cup fresh cilantro, chopped

Directions:

1. For the marinade: place all the ingredients except the chicken breasts in a large bowl and mix until well combined.
2. Add the chicken breasts and mix well.
3. Refrigerate to marinate for about 6-8 hours.
4. Remove the chicken breasts from bowl, reserving marinade.
5. Add the oil in the Instant Pot and select "Sauté". Now, add 4 chicken breasts, skin side down and cook for about 4-5 minutes or until golden brown.
6. With a slotted spoon, transfer the chicken breasts onto a plate.
7. Repeat with the remaining chicken breasts.
8. For sauce: in the pot, add the sugar and cook until the sugar begins to melt, stirring continuously.
9. Add the chicken broth with the reserved marinade and with a spatula, scrape the brown bits from the bottom.
10. Select the "Cancel" and stir in the chicken breasts.
11. Secure the lid and turn to "Seal" position.
12. Select "Poultry" and just use the default time of 20 minutes.
13. Press the "Cancel" and allow a "Natural" release.
14. Carefully remove the lid and serve hot with the garnishing of cilantro.

Nutrition Information

- Calories: 371
- Fat: 14.4g
- Saturated Fat: 3.3g
- Cholesterol: 126mg
- Sodium: 1032mg
- Carbohydrates: 16g
- Fiber: 0.8g
- Sugar: 13.1g
- Protein: 42.2g

MARINATED CHICKEN CURRY

Servings: 8

Prep Time: 36 minutes

Ingredients:

For Chicken Marinade:

- 1 tablespoon fresh ginger, grated
- 6 garlic cloves, minced finely
- 1 tablespoon yellow curry powder
- Salt, as required
- 3 pounds skinless, boneless chicken thighs, cut into pieces

For Curry:

- 2 tablespoons coconut oil
- 1 large onion, chopped
- 3 tablespoons all-purpose flour
- 2 fresh lemongrass stalks, sliced into 3-inch pieces and pounded
- 4 tablespoons yellow curry powder
- 1 bay leaf
- 4 tablespoons fish sauce
- 4 teaspoons granulated sugar
- Salt, as required
- 2 (13½-ounce) cans coconut milk
- 6 red potatoes, peeled and cut into bite sized pieces
- 6 medium carrots, peeled and cut into bite sized pieces
- 2 scallions (green part), chopped

Directions:

1. For the marinade: place all the ingredients except the chicken breasts in a large bowl and mix until well combined.
2. Add the chicken pieces and coat with marinade generously.
3. Refrigerate to marinate for about 1-2 hours.
4. Add the oil in the Instant Pot and select "Sauté". Now, add the chicken pieces and cook or about 5 minutes.
5. With the spoon, push the chicken to one side of the pot.
6. In the pot, add the onions and cook for about 3 minutes.
7. Stir in the four and cook for about 2 minutes, stirring continuously.
8. Select "Cancel" and stir in the lemongrass pieces, curry powder, bay leaf, fish sauce, sugar and coconut milk.
9. Secure the lid and turn to "Seal" position.
10. Cook on "Manual" with "High Pressure" for about 2 minutes.
11. Press the "Cancel" and allow a "Natural" release for about 5 minutes and then, allow a "Quick" release.
12. Carefully remove the lid and add the potatoes and carrots.
13. Secure the lid and turn to "Seal" position.
14. Cook on "Manual" with "High Pressure" for about 4 minutes.
15. Press the "Cancel" and allow a "Natural" release for about 5 minutes and then, allow a "Quick" release.
16. Carefully, remove the lid and serve hot with the garnishing of scallions.

Nutrition Information

- Calories: 750
- Fat: 39.6g
- Saturated Fat: 26.8g
- Cholesterol: 151mg
- Sodium: 920mg
- Carbohydrates: 45g
- Fiber: 9.1g
- Sugar: 10.7g

- Protein: 56.2g

Chicken & Bell Pepper Curry

Servings: 4

Prep Time: 30 minutes

Ingredients:

- 2 (8-ounce) boneless, skinless chicken breasts
- 3 tablespoons fish sauce
- 2 tablespoons red curry paste
- 2 tablespoons brown sugar
- 1 (13½-ounce) can full-fat coconut milk
- 3 cups mixed bell peppers, seeded and julienned
- 1 cup red onion, sliced and
- 1 tablespoon fresh lime juice

Directions:

1. In the pot of Instant Pot, place chicken, curry paste, brown sugar, fish sauce and coconut milk and stir to combine.
2. Secure the lid and turn to "Seal" position.
3. Cook on "Manual" with "High Pressure" for about 8 minutes.
4. Press the "Cancel" and allow a "Quick" release.
5. Carefully remove the lid of Instant Pot and with a spoon, place the chicken breasts into a bowl.
6. Select "Sauté" and stir in bell peppers, onion and lime juice.
7. Cook for about 3-5 minutes.
8. Meanwhile, cut the chicken breasts into bite sized pieces.
9. Add the chicken meat into pot and stir to combine.
10. Select the "Cancel" and serve hot.

Nutrition Information

- Calories: 548
- Fat: 35.9g
- Saturated Fat: 22.5g
- Cholesterol: 101mg
- Sodium: 1159mg
- Carbohydrates: 21.8g
- Fiber: 3.9g
- Sugar: 13.8g
- Protein: 37.3g

LEMONGRASS CHICKEN

Servings: 5

Prep Time: 35 minutes

Ingredients:

- 1 thick lemongrass stalk, papery outer skins and rough bottom removed, trimmed to the bottom 5-inch
- 1 tablespoon fresh ginger, chopped
- 4 garlic cloves, crushed
- 3 tablespoons soy sauce
- 2 tablespoons fish sauce
- 1 cup full-fat coconut milk
- 10 (4-ounce) skinless chicken drumsticks
- Salt and ground black pepper, as required
- 1 teaspoon coconut oil
- 1 large onion, sliced thinly
- 2 tablespoons fresh lime juice

Directions:

1. In a food processor, add the lemongrass, ginger, garlic, soy sauce and fish sauce and pulse until a smooth sauce forms.
2. Sprinkle the chicken drumsticks with salt and pepper evenly.
3. Add the oil in the Instant Pot and select "Sauté". Now, add the onion and cook for about 4-5 minutes.
4. Select the "Cancel" and place the drumsticks, followed by the sauce.
5. Secure the lid and turn to "Seal" position.

6. Cook on "Manual" with "High Pressure" for about 15 minutes.
7. Press the "Cancel" and allow a "Quick" release.
8. Carefully remove the lid and mix in the lime juice.
9. Serve hot.

Nutrition Information

- Calories: 530
- Fat: 25.4g
- Saturated Fat: 14.4g
- Cholesterol: 200mg
- Sodium: 1300mg
- Carbohydrates: 8.3g
- Fiber: 2g
- Sugar: 3.4g
- Protein: 65g

GLAZED CHICKEN BREASTS

Servings: 3

Prep Time: 25 minutes

Ingredients:

- 2 (7-ounce) boneless, skinless chicken breasts
- 2 tablespoons fresh ginger, grated
- 1 garlic clove, minced
- 1/3 cup chicken broth
- ¼ cup honey
- ¼ cup soy sauce
- 2 tablespoons fish sauce
- 1 tablespoon canola oil
- 2 teaspoons cornstarch
- 2 tablespoons water

Directions:

1. In the pot of Instant Pot, place all the ingredients except the cornstarch and water and stir to combine.
2. Secure the lid and turn to "Seal" position.
3. Cook on "Manual" with "High Pressure" for about 8 minutes.
4. Press the "Cancel" and allow a "Quick" release.
5. Meanwhile, in a bowl, add the cornstarch and water and mix well.
6. Carefully remove the lid and with the tongs, transfer the chicken breasts onto a plate.
7. Cut the chicken breasts into desired sized slices.
8. Add the cornstarch mixture into pot, stirring continuously.

9. Select "Sauté" and cook for about 1-2 minutes.
10. Select the "Cancel" and stir in the chicken slices.
11. Serve hot.

Nutrition Information

- Calories: 419
- Fat: 14.9g
- Saturated Fat: 3.2g
- Cholesterol: 118mg
- Sodium: 2300mg
- Carbohydrates: 29.9g
- Fiber: 0.7g
- Sugar: 24.2g
- Protein: 41.2g

MEAT RECIPES

BRAISED BEEF BRISKET

Servings: 8

Prep Time: 1½hours

Ingredients:

- 1 tablespoon sesame oil
- 1 small onion, sliced
- 1 tablespoon fresh ginger, minced
- 4 garlic cloves, smashed
- 1 (2½-pound) beef brisket
- ½ cup hoisin sauce
- 3 tablespoons fish sauce
- 2 tablespoons hot sauce
- ¼ cup water
- Salt and ground black pepper, as required

Directions:

1. Add the oil in the Instant Pot and select "Sauté". Now, add the onion and cook for about 1-2 minutes.
2. Add the ginger and garlic and cook for about 2 minutes.
3. Select the "Cancel" and stir in the remaining ingredients.
4. Secure the lid and turn to "Seal" position.
5. Cook on "Manual" with "High Pressure" for about 60 minutes.
6. Press the "Cancel" and allow a "Natural" release for about 10 minutes and then, allow a "Quick" release.
7. Carefully remove the lid and place the brisket onto a cutting board for about 5-10 minutes.
8. Select "Sauté" and cook for about 10 minutes or until desired thickness of cooking sauce.
9. Cut the brisket into thin pieces against the grain.
10. Serve the brisket slices with alongside the sauce.

Nutrition Information

- Calories: 324
- Fat: 11.1g
- Saturated Fat: 3.7g
- Cholesterol: 127mg
- Sodium: 988mg
- Carbohydrates: 9.2g
- Fiber: 0.8g
- Sugar: 5.1g
- Protein: 44.2g

Shredded Chuck Roast

Servings: 6

Prep Time: 50 minutes

Ingredients:

- ¼ cup soy sauce
- 2 tablespoons fresh lime juice
- 2 tablespoons fresh apple juice
- 2 tablespoons rice vinegar
- 1 tablespoon curry paste
- 1 tablespoon fresh ginger, minced
- 1 tablespoon garlic, minced
- Salt, as required
- 1 tablespoon canola oil
- 1 jalapeño pepper, chopped
- 2 pounds beef chuck roast, cubed

Directions:

1. For sauce: in a bowl, add all the ingredients except the oil, jalapeño pepper and roast and beat until well combined.
2. Add the oil in the Instant Pot and select "Sauté". Now, add the jalapeño pepper and cook for about 1-2 minutes.
3. Add the chuck roast and cook for about 1-2 minutes.
4. Select the "Cancel" and place the sauce on top.
5. Secure the lid and turn to "Seal" position.
6. Cook on "Manual" with "High Pressure" for about 30 minutes.
7. Meanwhile, preheat the oven to broiler and line a baking sheet with a foil piece.

8. Press the "Cancel" and allow a "Natural" release for about 10 minutes and then, allow a "Quick" release.
9. Carefully remove the lid and with 2 forks, shred the meat.
10. Mix the meat with sauce and serve

Nutrition Information

- Calories: 639
- Fat: 46g
- Saturated Fat: 17g
- Cholesterol: 156mg
- Sodium: 727mg
- Carbohydrates: 12.1g
- Fiber: 0.5g
- Sugar: 8.3g
- Protein: 40.6g

CARAMELIZED PORK

Servings: 6

Prep Time: 55 minutes

Ingredients:

- 2 tablespoons canola oil
- 2 pounds pork butt, cut in 1-inch pieces
- Salt and ground black pepper, as required
- 4 tablespoons brown sugar
- 3 garlic cloves, minced
- 2 tablespoons fish sauce
- ½ cup chicken broth
- ½ cup water
- 1 small onion, sliced
- 1 scallion (green part), chopped

Directions:

1. Add the oil in the Instant Pot and select "Sauté". Now, add the pork, salt and black pepper and cook for about 3-4 minutes or until browned completely.
2. Add the brown sugar and cook for about 2 minutes or until pork turn a golden brown color, stirring continuously.
3. Stir in the garlic and cook for about 1 minutes.
4. Select the "Cancel" and stir in the fish sauce, broth and water.
5. Secure the lid and turn to "Seal" position.
6. Cook on "Manual" with "High Pressure" for about 20 minutes.

7. Press the "Cancel" and allow a "Natural" release for about 10 minutes and then, allow a "Quick" release.
8. Carefully remove the lid and select "Sauté".
9. Stir in the onions and cook for about 5-10 minutes or until desired thickness of sauce.
10. Select the "Cancel" and serve with the garnishing of scallion.

Nutrition Information

- Calories: 369
- Fat: 14.9g
- Saturated Fat: 3.7g
- Cholesterol: 139mg
- Sodium: 624mg
- Carbohydrates: 8g
- Fiber: 0.4g
- Sugar: 6.7g
- Protein: 48.1g

BRAISED PORK BELLY

Servings: 8

Prep Time: 55 minutes

Ingredients:

- 2 shallots, chopped finely
- 3 garlic cloves, minced
- 2 tablespoons fish sauce
- 1 teaspoon thick soy sauce
- Salt and ground black pepper, as required
- 2½ pounds lean pork belly, cut into 1-inch squares
- 7 tablespoons granulated sugar
- 2 cups coconut water
- 1 scallion (green part), chopped

Directions:

1. In a large bowl, add the shallots, garlic, fish sauce, soy sauce, salt and black pepper and mix until well combined.
2. Stir in the pork pieces and coat with the mixture generously.
3. Place the sugar in the Instant Pot and select "Sauté". Cook for about 10-15 minutes or until sugar starts to become dark in color, stirring frequently.
4. Add the pork belly pieces and cook for about 5 minutes, stirring continuously.
5. Select the "Cancel" and stir in the coconut water.
6. Secure the lid and turn to "Seal" position.
7. Cook on "Manual" with "High Pressure" for about 35 minutes.

8. Press the "Cancel" and allow a "Natural" release for about 15 minutes and then, allow a "Quick" release.
9. Carefully remove the lid and serve with the garnishing of scallion.

Nutrition Information

- Calories: 713
- Fat: 38.3g
- Saturated Fat: 16.5g
- Cholesterol: 164mg
- Sodium: 2700mg
- Carbohydrates: 14.3g
- Fiber: 0.7g
- Sugar: 12.3g
- Protein: 66.3g

SHREDDED PORK

Servings: 8

Prep Time: 1¼ hours

Ingredients:

- 1 tablespoon garlic, minced
- ¼ cup fish sauce
- 1 tablespoon fresh lime juice
- 2 tablespoons sugar
- 1 teaspoon five-spice powder
- Freshly ground black pepper, as required
- 2½ pounds pork butt
- 1 tablespoon canola oil

Directions:

1. For sauce: in a bowl, add all the ingredients except the oil and pork and beat until well combined.
2. In the pot of the Instant Pot, place the pork butt and top with the sauce evenly.
3. Secure the lid and turn to "Seal" position.
4. Cook on "Manual" with "High Pressure" for about 60 minutes.
5. Press the "Cancel" and allow a "Natural" release.
6. Carefully remove the lid and with a spoon, place the pork butt into a bowl.
7. With 2 forks, shred the meat.
8. In a large skillet, heat oil over medium heat and stir in the shredded meat.

9. Add desired amount of cooking liquid and cook for about 1-2 minutes.
10. Serve hot.

Nutrition Information

- Calories: 305
- Fat: 11.2g
- Saturated Fat: 3.3g
- Cholesterol: 130mg
- Sodium: 774mg
- Carbohydrates: 3.7g
- Fiber: 0g
- Sugar: 3.3g
- Protein: 44.7g

FISH RECIPES

STEAMED SEA BASS

Servings: 4

Prep Time: 20 minutes

Ingredients:

For Sea Bass:

- 1 teaspoon fresh ginger, minced
- 1 teaspoon garlic, minced
- 1 tablespoon rice wine
- 1 tablespoon soy sauce
- 1 tablespoon fish sauce
- Freshly ground black pepper, as required
- 1 pound whole sea bass
- 2 cups water

For Sauce:

- 1 teaspoon fresh ginger, julienned finely
- ¼ cup light soy sauce
- 1 tablespoon rice wine
- 1 tablespoon water
- 1 scallion, julienned
- ¼ cup canola oil

Directions:

1. For marinade: in a baking dish, add all the ingredients except the fish and water and mix well.

2. Add the fish and mix well.
3. Set aside for about 20-30 minutes.
4. In the bottom of Instant Pot, arrange a steamer basket and pour water.
5. Place the fish in steamer basket.
6. Secure the lid and turn to "Seal" position.
7. Cook on "Manual" with "Low Pressure" for about 2 minutes.
8. Press the "Cancel" and allow a "Quick" release.
9. Meanwhile, in a small bowl, add the ginger, soy sauce, wine, and 1 tablespoon of water and mix well.
10. Carefully remove the lid and transfer the fish onto a serving platter.
11. Place the ginger mixture over the fish.
12. Now, arrange the scallion over the fish.
13. In a frying pan, add the oil over medium heat and cook until just heated.
14. Pour oil over the fish and serve.

Nutrition Information

- Calories: 372
- Fat: 18.7g
- Saturated Fat: 2g
- Cholesterol: 46mg
- Sodium: 1683mg
- Carbohydrates: 27.3g
- Fiber: 0.3g
- Sugar: 15.8g
- Protein: 23.9g

CARAMELIZED SALMON

Servings: 4

Prep Time: 20 minutes

Ingredients:

- 1/3 cup light brown sugar
- 3 tablespoons fish sauce
- 1 tablespoon coconut oil, melted
- 1 tablespoon fresh lime juice
- 1½ tablespoons soy sauce
- 1 teaspoon fresh ginger, grated
- 1 teaspoon fresh lime zest, grated
- Freshly ground black pepper, as required
- 4 (6-ounce) skinless salmon fillets
- 1 scallion (green part), chopped

Directions:

1. Place all the ingredients except the salmon and scallion in a bowl and mix until well combined.
2. Place the sugar mixture in the Instant Pot and select "Sauté". Cook for about 2-3 minutes, stirring frequently.
3. Select the "Cancel" and stir in the salmon fillets.
4. Secure the lid and turn to "Seal" position.
5. Cook on "Manual" with "Low Pressure" for about 1 minute.
6. Press the "Cancel" and allow a "Natural" release for about 5 minutes and then, allow a "Quick" release.
7. Carefully remove the lid and select "Sauté".

8. Cook for about 1 minute.
9. With a slotted spoon, transfer the salmon fillets onto a platter.
10. Cook the sauce for about 3 minutes.
11. Select the "Cancel" and pour the caramel sauce over the salmon fillets.
12. Serve with the garnishing of the scallion.

Nutrition Information

- Calories: 388
- Fat: 21.5g
- Saturated Fat: 6.7g
- Cholesterol: 98mg
- Sodium: 1482mg
- Carbohydrates: 13.5g
- Fiber: 0.3g
- Sugar: 12.4g
- Protein: 34.4g

CATFISH IN CARAMEL SAUCE

Servings: 4

Prep Time: 20 minutes

Ingredients:

- 3 garlic cloves, minced and divided
- 2 scallions (white part), minced
- 3 tablespoons fish sauce
- 1 tablespoon sugar
- ½ teaspoon coconut caramel sauce
- Freshly ground black pepper, as required
- 1 pound catfish fillets
- 1 tablespoon coconut oil
- 1 shallot, minced
- ½ cup coconut water

Directions:

1. Place half of the garlic, scallions, fish sauce, sugar, caramel sauce and black pepper in a large bowl and mix well.
2. Add the fish and coat with mixture generously.
3. Set aside to marinate for about 15-30 minutes.
4. Add the oil in the Instant Pot and select "Sauté". Now, add the shallot and remaining garlic and cook for about 1 minute.
5. Add the fish with marinade sauce and cook for about 2 minutes.
6. Flip the fish and cook for about 2 minutes.
7. Select the "Cancel" and stir in the coconut water.
8. Secure the lid and turn to "Seal" position.

9. Cook on "Manual" with "Low Pressure" for about 3 minutes.
10. Press the "Cancel" and allow a "Quick" release.
11. Carefully, remove the lid and select "Sauté".
12. Cook for about 3-5 minutes, occasionally pouring the sauce over the fish.
13. Select the "Cancel" and serve.

Nutrition Information

- Calories: 178
- Fat: 17.5g
- Saturated Fat: 4.2g
- Cholesterol: 58mg
- Sodium: 1100mg
- Carbohydrates: 8.4g
- Fiber: 0.6g
- Sugar: 4.5g
- Protein: 22.1g

FISH CURRY

Servings: 4

Prep Time: 20 minutes

Ingredients:

- 1 (14½-ounce) can coconut milk
- 2 tablespoons fresh lime juice
- 2 teaspoons Sriracha
- 1 teaspoon soy sauce
- 1 teaspoon fish sauce
- 1 teaspoon honey
- 2 garlic cloves, minced
- 1 tablespoon curry paste
- 1 teaspoon ground ginger
- 1 teaspoon ground turmeric
- Salt and ground white pepper, as required
- 1 pound sea bass, cut into 1-inch cubes
- ¼ cup fresh cilantro, chopped

Directions:

1. In a large bowl, add the coconut milk, lime juice, Sriracha, soy sauce, fish sauce, honey, garlic, curry paste, ginger, turmeric, salt and white pepper and beat until well combined.
2. In the pot of Instant Pot, place the fish pieces and top with the sauce.
3. Secure the lid and turn to "Seal" position.
4. Cook on "Manual" with "High Pressure" for about 3 minutes.

5. Press the "Cancel" and allow a "Quick" release.
6. Carefully remove the lid and serve with the garnishing of cilantro.

Nutrition Information

- Calories: 473
- Fat: 37.2g
- Saturated Fat: 23.9g
- Cholesterol: 0mg
- Sodium: 264mg
- Carbohydrates: 10.2g
- Fiber: 3.1g
- Sugar: 5.1g
- Protein: 28.1g

Fish & Veggie Curry

Servings: 6

Prep Time: 1½ hours

Ingredients:

- 1½ pounds catfish fillets
- 2 cups carrots, peeled and sliced
- 1 red bell pepper, seeded and sliced
- 1 medium zucchini, chopped
- 2 tablespoons green curry paste
- 1 tablespoon fish sauce
- 2 (14-ounce) cans coconut milk
- 2 cups water

Directions:

1. In the pot of Instant Pot, add all the ingredients and stir to combine.
2. Secure the lid and turn to "Seal" position.
3. Select "Soup" and just use the default time of 60 minutes.
4. Press the "Cancel" and allow a "Quick" release.
5. Carefully remove the lid and serve hot.

Nutrition Information

- Calories: 500
- Fat: 41.3g
- Saturated Fat: 29.6g
- Cholesterol: 53mg
- Sodium: 543mg
- Carbohydrates: 15.1g

- Fiber: 4.4g
- Sugar: 7.9g
- Protein: 21.7g

RICE RECIPES

COCONUT RICE WITH PEAS

Servings: 6

Prep Time: 15 minutes

Ingredients:

- 2 cups jasmine rice
- 1 (15-ounce) can lite coconut milk
- ½ cup water
- 1 cup frozen peas, thawed
- 1 tablespoon fresh lime juice
- 2 tablespoons fresh cilantro, chopped

Directions:

1. In the pot of Instant Pot, add the rice coconut milk and water and stir to combine.
2. Secure the lid and turn to "Seal" position.
3. Cook on "Manual" with "High Pressure" for about 4 minutes.
4. Press the "Cancel" and allow a "Natural" release.
5. Carefully remove the lid and immediately, stir in the peas and lime juice.
6. Serve with the garnishing of cilantro.

Nutrition Information

- Calories: 397
- Fat: 17g
- Saturated Fat: 15g
- Cholesterol: 0mg
- Sodium: 31mg
- Carbohydrates: 55.8g
- Fiber: 5.7g
- Sugar: 3.6g
- Protein: 7g

VEGGIE RICE

Servings: 4

Prep Time: 25 minutes

Ingredients:

- 4 teaspoons vegetable oil, divided
- ½ cup onion, chopped finely
- 1 tablespoon fresh ginger, minced finely
- 2 teaspoons garlic, minced finely
- 1½ cups jasmine rice, rinsed
- ¾ cup frozen peas
- ¾ cup frozen carrots
- 3 tablespoons soy sauce
- 1 tablespoon oyster sauce
- ½ teaspoon sesame oil
- Freshly ground black pepper, as required
- 1¾ cups water
- 2 eggs, beaten

Directions:

1. Place 1 tablespoon of the vegetable oil in the Instant Pot and select "Sauté". Now, add the onion and cook for about 2 minutes.
2. Stir in the ginger and garlic and cook for about 1 minute.
3. Select the "Cancel" and stir in the remaining ingredients except the eggs.
4. Secure the lid and turn to "Seal" position.
5. Cook on "Manual" with "High Pressure" for about 5 minutes.
6. Press the "Cancel" and allow a "Natural" release for about 10 minutes and then, allow a "Quick" release.
7. Carefully remove the lid and let the rice rest for a few minutes.
8. Meanwhile, in a nonstick frying pan, heat the remaining oil over medium heat and cook the beaten eggs for about 2 minutes or until scrambled, staring continuously.
9. Add the scrambles eggs into the pot with the rice and stir to combine.
10. Serve immediately.

Nutrition Information

- Calories: 368
- Fat: 7.5g
- Saturated Fat: 1.7g
- Cholesterol: 82mg
- Sodium: 772mg
- Carbohydrates: 64.3g
- Fiber: 5.8g
- Sugar: 3.5g
- Protein: 10.1g

CHICKEN RICE

Servings: 8

Prep Time: 45 minutes

Ingredients:

For Chicken:

- 1 (5-pound) whole chicken, trimmed and cut in half
- 1 onion, halved
- 1 (2¼-inch) piece fresh ginger, cut in half
- 1 teaspoon ground turmeric
- Salt, as required
- 9 cups boiling water

For Dressing:

- 4 tablespoons water
- 2 tablespoons rice vinegar
- 2 tablespoons sugar
- ½ white onion, sliced thinly

For Rice:

- 3 tablespoons canola oil
- 5 garlic cloves, minced
- 2½ cups jasmine rice, rinsed
- ½ cup sweet rice, rinsed
- ½ teaspoon ground turmeric
- Salt, as required

- ½ cup fresh cilantro, chopped

For Sauce:

- 4 tablespoons sugar
- 3 tablespoons fresh lime juice
- 3 tablespoons fish sauce
- 5 garlic cloves, mashed
- ¼ teaspoon fresh ginger, julienned

Directions:

1. In the pot of Instant Pot, place the chicken alongside the onion, ginger, turmeric, salt and billing water.
2. Secure the lid and turn to "Seal" position.
3. Cook on "Manual" with "High Pressure" for about 10 minutes.
4. Press the "Cancel" and allow a "Natural" release for about 5 minutes and then, allow a "Quick" release.
5. Meanwhile, for dressing: in a bowl, add the water, vinegar and sugar and mix well.
6. Stir in the onion slices and set aside for about 15 minutes.
7. Carefully remove the lid and place the chicken onto a platter to cool.
8. Through a sieve, strain the broth into a bowl and remove the solids.
9. With paper towels, wipe the inner pot of Instant Pot.
10. Add the oil in the Instant Pot and select "Sauté". Now, add the garlic and cook for about 1 minute.
11. Add the jasmine rice and sweet rice and sauté for about 4 minutes.
12. Select the "Cancel" and stir in 3 cups of the broth, turmeric and 1 teaspoon of the salt.
13. Secure the lid and turn to "Seal" position.
14. Cook on "Manual" with "Low Pressure" for about 12 minutes.
15. Press the "Cancel" and allow a "Quick" release.
16. Meanwhile, for the sauce: place all the ingredients in a bowl and mix well.

17. Carefully remove the lid and transfer the rice onto a platter.
18. Meanwhile, remove the bone from the chicken and shred the meat.
19. In a large bowl, add the shredded meat, onion mixture and cilantro and mix well.
20. Divide the rice and chicken mixture onto serving plates.
21. Top with the sauce and serve.

Nutrition Information

- Calories: 887
- Fat: 26.4g
- Saturated Fat: 6.2g
- Cholesterol: 252mg
- Sodium: 787mg
- Carbohydrates: 68.2g
- Fiber: 3.5g
- Sugar: 10.5g
- Protein: 87.4g

Chicken & Rice Porridge

Servings: 4

Prep Time: 40 minutes

Ingredients:

- 4 chicken leg quarters
- 1 white onion
- 2 shallots
- 1 (1-inch) piece fresh ginger, halved
- 8-10 cups boiling water
- 4 tablespoons chicken soup base, divided
- ¾ cup jasmine rice, rinsed
- ¼ cup sweet rice, rinsed
- 1 teaspoon fish sauce
- ½ teaspoon sugar
- Salt, as required
- 2 scallions (green part), chopped

Directions:

1. In the pot of Instant Pot, place the chicken, onion, shallot, ginger, 2 tablespoons of the chicken soup base and billing water.
2. Secure the lid and turn to "Seal" position.
3. Cook on "Manual" with "High Pressure" for about 8 minutes.
4. Press the "Cancel" and allow a "Natural" release for about 5 minutes and then, allow a "Quick" release.
5. Carefully remove the lid and place the chicken into the bowl of the cold water.
6. Drain the chicken and set aside to cool.

7. With a slotted spoon, remove the onion and shallots from the broth.
8. In the pot, add the rice and remaining chicken soup base and stir to combine.
9. Secure the lid and turn to "Seal" position.
10. Select "Porridge" and just use the default time of 18 minutes.
11. Meanwhile, remove the bone from the chicken and shred the meat.
12. Press the "Cancel" and allow a "Natural" release.
13. Carefully remove the lid and mix in the shredded meat, fish sauce, sugar and salt.
14. Serve with the garnishing of scallion.

Nutrition Information

- Calories: 379
- Fat: 13.1g
- Saturated Fat: 3.5g
- Cholesterol: 85mg
- Sodium: 1000mg
- Carbohydrates: 42.5g
- Fiber: 2.6g
- Sugar: 2.2g
- Protein: 22.8g

FISH CONGEE

Servings: 4

Prep Time: 40 minutes

Ingredients:

- ¾ cup rice, rinsed and drained
- 1½ pounds fish bones, scrubbed, rinsed and drained
- 1 shallot, halved
- 1 (½-inch) piece fresh ginger, sliced thinly
- 1 tablespoon fish sauce
- Salt, as required
- 6 cups boiling water
- Freshly ground black pepper, as required
- 1 pound grouper fillet, cut into ½-inch thick pieces
- 2 tablespoons fresh cilantro, chopped

Directions:

1. In the pot of Instant Pot, place all the ingredients except the fish fillets and cilantro.
2. Secure the lid and turn to "Seal" position.
3. Select "Porridge" and just use the default time of 20 minutes.
4. Press the "Cancel" and allow a "Natural" release.
5. Meanwhile, Sprinkle the fish pieces with a pinch of salt and black pepper.
6. Carefully remove the lid and select "Sauté".
7. With a slotted spoon, remove the fish bones.
8. Add the fish pieces and cook for about 2-3 minutes.

9. Select the "Cancel" and serve hot with the garnishing of cilantro.

Nutrition Information

- Calories: 266
- Fat: 1.7g
- Saturated Fat: 0.4g
- Cholesterol: 53mg
- Sodium: 460mg
- Carbohydrates: 28.9g
- Fiber: 0.5g
- Sugar: 0.2g
- Protein: 31g

SIDE DISHES RECIPES

GLAZED CHICKEN WINGS

Servings: 6

Prep Time: 40 minutes

Ingredients:

- 1 cup water
- 2 pounds chicken wings
- ¼ cup sugar
- ¼ cup fish sauce
- 3 garlic cloves, crushed
- 2 tablespoons canola oil
- 5 garlic cloves, minced

Directions:

1. In the bottom of Instant Pot, arrange a steamer trivet and pour 1 cup of water.
2. Arrange the chicken wings on top of the trivet in a single layer.
3. Secure the lid and turn to "Seal" position.
4. Cook on "Manual" with "High Pressure" for about 5 minutes.
5. Meanwhile, preheat the oven to broiler. Line a baking sheet with a piece of foil.
6. Press the "Cancel" and allow a "Quick" release.
7. Carefully remove the lid and transfer the wings onto a plate.

8. With paper towels, pat the chicken wings dry.
9. For sauce: in a large bowl, add the sugar, fish sauce and crushed garlic cloves and mix well.
10. Add the wings and coat with the sauce generously.
11. Remove the wings from the bowl, reserving any remaining sauce.
12. Arrange the wings onto the prepared baking sheet and broil for about 5 minutes per side.
13. Remove the wings from the oven and set aside.
14. In a skillet, heat the oil over medium heat and sauté the minced garlic for about 1-2 minutes.
15. Add the wings and reserved sauce and cook for about 1 minute, stirring continuously.
16. Serve hot.

Nutrition Information

- Calories: 370
- Fat: 15.9g
- Saturated Fat: 3,4g
- Cholesterol: 135mg
- Sodium: 1050mg
- Carbohydrates: 10.1g
- Fiber: 0.1g
- Sugar: 8.8g
- Protein: 44.6g

Zesty Meatballs

Servings: 8

Prep Time: 420 minutes

Ingredients:

For Meatballs:

- 1½ pounds ground pork
- 2 tablespoons fresh ginger, grated
- 1 tablespoon garlic, minced
- 1 tablespoon lemongrass paste
- 1 teaspoon fresh lime zest, grated
- 2 tablespoons fresh lime juice
- 1 tablespoon soy sauce
- ½ tablespoon chili paste
- Salt, as required

For Cooking:

- 1½ cups beef broth
- 1 tablespoon soy sauce
- ½ tablespoon fish sauce

Direction:

1. For meatballs: in a large bowl, add all the ingredients and with your hands, mix until well combined.
2. Make golf ball sized meatballs from the mixture and arrange onto a large parchment paper lined baking sheet.
3. Freeze or about 20 minutes.

4. In the pot of Instant Pot, place the meatballs and top with broth, soy sauce and fish sauce.
5. Secure the lid and turn to "Seal" position.
6. Cook on "Manual" with "High Pressure" for about 5 minutes.
7. Press the "Cancel" and allow a "Natural" release for about 10 minutes and then, allow a "Quick" release.
8. Carefully remove the lid and serve.

Nutrition Information

- Calories: 467
- Fat: 11.5g
- Saturated Fat: 3.8g
- Cholesterol: 228mg
- Sodium: 674mg
- Carbohydrates: 2.4g
- Fiber: 0.3g
- Sugar: 0.7g
- Protein: 83.1g

GARLICKY SPINACH

Servings: 4

Prep Time: 15 minutes

Ingredients:

- 2 tablespoons vegetable oil
- 1 tablespoon garlic, chopped finely
- 1¼ pounds fresh spinach
- 2 tablespoons fish sauce
- 2 tablespoons water
- Salt and ground black pepper, as required

Directions:

1. Add the oil in the Instant Pot and select "Sauté". Now, add the garlic and cook for about 1 minute.
2. Select the "Cancel" and stir in the spinach, fish sauce, water, salt and black pepper.
3. Secure the lid and turn to "Seal" position.
4. Select "Steam" and just use the default time of 1 minute.
5. Press the "Cancel" and allow a "Quick" release.
6. Carefully remove the lid and select the "Sauté".
7. Cook for about 1-2 minutes.
8. Select the "Cancel" and serve hot.

Nutrition Information

- Calories: 99
- Fat: 7.4g
- Saturated Fat: 1.4g
- Cholesterol: 0mg

- Sodium: 846mg
- Carbohydrates: 6.2g
- Fiber: 3.2g
- Sugar: 1g
- Protein: 4.6g

Soy Sauce Braised Broccoli

Servings: 4

Prep Time: 20 minutes

Ingredients:

- 1 cup water
- 4 cups broccoli florets
- 1 tablespoon peanut oil
- 4 garlic cloves, minced
- 1 teaspoon fresh ginger, grated
- 1 tablespoon soy sauce
- ½ tablespoon fish sauce
- ½ tablespoon rice wine

Directions:

1. In the bottom of Instant Pot, arrange a steamer basket and pour water.
2. Place the broccoli florets in steamer basket.
3. Secure the lid and turn to "Seal" position.
4. Cook on "Manual" with "High Pressure" for about 3-4 minutes.
5. Press the "Cancel" and allow a "Quick" release.
6. Carefully remove the lid and transfer the broccoli onto a plate.
7. Remove the steamer basket and water and with paper towels, pat the pot dry.
8. Add the oil in the Instant Pot and select "Sauté". Now, add the garlic and ginger and sauté for about 30 seconds.
9. Add broccoli and remaining ingredients and cook for about 1-2 minutes.

10. Select the "Cancel" and serve hot.

Nutrition Information

- Calories: 73
- Fat: 3.7g
- Saturated Fat: 0.6g
- Cholesterol: 0mg
- Sodium: 446mg
- Carbohydrates: 8g
- Fiber: 2.5g
- Sugar: 2.3g
- Protein: 3.1g

SAUTÉED MUSHROOMS

Servings: 6

Prep Time: 25 minutes

Ingredients:

- 1 tablespoon vegetable oil
- 2 garlic cloves, chopped finely
- 1 red chili, chopped
- 24 ounces fresh mushrooms, sliced
- 2 tablespoons water
- 2 tablespoons soy sauce
- 1 tablespoon fish sauce
- Freshly ground black pepper, as required

Directions:

1. Add the oil in the Instant Pot and select "Sauté". Now, add garlic and red chili and cook for about 1 minute.
2. Add the mushrooms and cook for about 1-2 minutes.
3. Select the "Cancel" and stir in remaining ingredients.
4. Secure the lid and turn to "Seal" position.
5. Select "Steam" and just use the default time of 2 minutes.
6. Press the "Cancel" and allow a "Quick" release.
7. Carefully remove the lid and select "Sauté".
8. Cook for about 3-4 minutes.
9. Select the "Cancel" and serve hot.

Nutrition Information

- Calories: 50
- Fat: 2.6g

- Saturated Fat: 0.5g
- Cholesterol: 0mg
- Sodium: 539mg
- Carbohydrates: 4.7g
- Fiber: 1.2g
- Sugar: 2.2g
- Protein: 4.1g

Salads & Eggs Recipes

Chicken & Veggie Salad

Servings: 4

Prep Time: 35 minutes

Ingredients:

For Chicken:

- 2 (8-ounce) boneless, skinless chicken breasts
- Salt, as required
- 1 cup water

For Dressing:

- 1/3 cup fish sauce
- 1/3 cup fresh lime juice
- 2 red chilies, seeded and chopped finely
- 2 tablespoons brown sugar

For Salad:

- 2 carrots, peeled and cut into matchsticks
- ½ large head cabbage, shredded finely
- 1 cup fresh cilantro leaves
- 1 cup fresh mint leaves

Directions:

1. For chicken: Lightly sprinkle the chicken breasts with salt..

2. In the bottom of Instant Pot, arrange a steamer trivet and pour the water.
3. Place the chicken breasts on top of the trivet.
4. Secure the lid and turn to "Seal" position.
5. Cook on "Manual" with "High Pressure" for about 12 minutes.
6. Press the "Cancel" and allow a "Quick" release.
7. Carefully remove the lid and transfer the chicken breasts onto a cutting board.
8. Chop the chicken breasts into desired sized pieces.
9. For dressing: in a bowl, add all the ingredients and beat until sugar is dissolved.
10. In a large serving bowl, place the chopped chicken and all salad ingredients and mix.
11. Pour the dressing and toss to coat.
12. Serve immediately.

Nutrition Information

- Calories: 293
- Fat: 8.7g
- Saturated Fat: 2.4g
- Cholesterol: 101mg
- Sodium: 2000mg
- Carbohydrates: 16.3g
- Fiber: 4.8g
- Sugar: 9.8g
- Protein: 36.3g

Chicken & Noodles Salad

Servings: 4

Prep Time: 40 minutes

Ingredients:

For Chicken:

- 1 pound chicken thighs
- Salt and ground black pepper, as required
- 1 tablespoon vegetable oil
- ½ cup water

For Dressing:

- 4 garlic cloves, chopped
- 1/3 cup vegetable oil
- 1/3 cup fresh lime juice
- ¼ cup fish sauce
- 2 tablespoons rice vinegar
- 2 tablespoons brown sugar
- 3 serrano peppers, sliced thinly

For Salad:

- 6 ounces rice noodles, soaked for 15 minutes and drained
- 2 cups carrots, peeled and julienned
- 2 cups cabbage, shredded
- 2 cups lettuce, shredded
- ½ cup fresh mint leaves, chopped

Directions:

1. For chicken: Sprinkle the chicken thighs with salt and black pepper.
2. Add the oil in the Instant Pot and select "Sauté". Now, add the chicken thighs and cook for about 1 minute per side.
3. Transfer the chicken thighs onto a plate.
4. In the bottom of Instant Pot, arrange a steamer trivet and pour the water.
5. Place the chicken thighs on top of the trivet.
6. Secure the lid and turn to "Seal" position.
7. Cook on "Manual" with "High Pressure" for about 9 minutes.
8. Press the "Cancel" and allow a "Natural" release for about 10 minutes and then, allow a "Quick" release.
9. Carefully remove the lid and transfer the chicken thighs onto a cutting board.
10. Chop the chicken thighs into desired sized pieces.
11. For the dressing: in a food processor, add all the ingredients except the Serrano peppers and pulse until smooth.
12. Transfer the dressing into a large serving bowl and stir in the Serrano pepper slices.
13. With a kitchen scissors, cut the drained noodles into shorter pieces.
14. In a large skillet, heat a small amount of the dressing over medium-high heat and stir-fry the noodles for about 5 minutes.
15. Remove from the heat and set aside.
16. In the bowl of the remaining dressing, add the chicken, salad ingredients and noodles and gently toss to coat.
17. Serve immediately.

Nutrition Information

- Calories: 548
- Fat: 32.5g
- Saturated Fat: 7g
- Cholesterol: 101mg
- Sodium: 1540mg

- Carbohydrates: 26.4g
- Fiber: 3.8g
- Sugar: 9.3g
- Protein: 35.8g

Beef Salad

Servings: 4

Prep Time: 20 minutes

Ingredients:

For Beef:

- 1 pound flank steaks, trimmed and cut into ¼-inch thick strips
- Freshly ground black pepper, as required
- ½ tablespoon canola oil
- 2 garlic cloves, minced
- ¼ cup water
- ¼ cup soy sauce
- 2 tablespoons fresh lime juice
- 1 tablespoon honey

For Dressing:

- 2 garlic cloves, crushed
- 2 red chilies, seeded and sliced finely
- 3 tablespoons fish sauce
- 3 tablespoons soy sauce
- 3 tablespoons fresh lime juice
- 3 tablespoons rice vinegar
- 2 tablespoons soft brown sugar

For Salad:

- 6 cups lettuce, shredded
- 2 cups carrots, peeled and shredded
- 1 large tomato, cubed

- 1 cucumber, peeled and sliced thinly
- ½ cup fresh cilantro, chopped
- ½ cup fresh mint, chopped

Directions:

1. Season steak evenly with black pepper..
2. Add the oil in the Instant Pot and select "Sauté". Now, add the steak, salt and black pepper and cook for about 5 minutes.
3. Transfer the steak into a bowl.
4. In the pot, add the garlic and cook for about 1 minute.
5. Select the "Cancel" and stir in beef, water, soy sauce, lemon juice and honey.
6. Secure the lid and turn to "Seal" position.
7. Cook on "Manual" with "High Pressure" for about 12 minutes.
8. Press the "Cancel" and allow a "Quick" release.
9. Carefully remove the lid and transfer the steak onto a plate.
10. For dressing: in a bowl, add all the ingredients and beat until sugar is dissolved.
11. In a large serving bowl, place the steak slices and all salad ingredients and mix.
12. Pour the dressing and toss to coat.
13. Serve immediately.

Nutrition Information

- Calories: 360
- Fat: 11.6g
- Saturated Fat: 4.1g
- Cholesterol: 15mg
- Sodium: 2700mg
- Carbohydrates: 26g
- Fiber: 4g
- Sugar: 15.8g
- Protein: 36.4g

Shrimp Salad

Servings: 4

Prep Time: 25 minutes

Ingredients:

For Shrimp:

- 1 cup water
- ¾ pound medium frozen shrimp, peeled and deveined
- 1 tablespoon butter, melted
- 2 tablespoons fresh lime juice
- Salt and ground black pepper, as required

For Dressing:

- 1/3 cup fresh mint
- 3 tablespoons red onion, chopped
- 1 garlic clove, peeled
- ¼ cup olive oil
- 2 tablespoons fresh lime juice
- 1 tablespoon rice vinegar
- 1 teaspoon fish sauce
- ¼ teaspoon honey
- 1/8 teaspoon chili paste

For Salad:

- 6 cups romaine lettuce, chopped
- 2 cups zucchini, julienned
- 2 cucumbers, sliced thinly
- 1 large carrot, peeled and julienned

- 1 red chili, sliced thinly
- ½ cup raw unsalted peanuts, toasted

Directions:

1. In the bottom of Instant Pot, arrange a steamer trivet and pour water
2. Arrange the shrimp on top of trivet in a single layer.
3. Drizzle with melted butter and lemon juice. Sprinkle with salt and black pepper.
4. Secure the lid and turn to "Seal" position.
5. Select "Steam" and just use the default time of 2 minutes.
6. Press the "Cancel" and allow a "Natural" release.
7. Carefully remove the lid and transfer the shrimp onto a plate.
8. For the dressing: in a food processor, add all the ingredients except the Serrano peppers and pulse until smooth.
9. In a large bowl, add all the salad ingredients and shrimp and mix well.
10. Drizzle with the dressing and toss to coat.
11. Serve immediately.

Nutrition Information

- Calories: 401
- Fat: 26.4g
- Saturated Fat: 5.4g
- Cholesterol: 187mg
- Sodium: 377mg
- Carbohydrates: 17.9g
- Fiber: 4.6g
- Sugar: 6.7g
- Protein: 26.8g

Chicken & Veggie Omelet

Servings: 3

Prep Time: 20 minutes

Ingredients:

- 5 eggs
- 2 tablespoons coconut milk
- 1 teaspoon fish sauce
- 1 garlic clove, chopped finely
- Salt and ground black pepper, as required
- 1 tablespoon vegetable oil
- 1/3 cup cooked chicken, shredded
- 1/3 cup mung bean sprouts
- ¼ cup mixed fresh herbs (mint, basil and cilantro leaves), chopped finely
- 1 scallion, chopped finely

Directions:

1. In a bowl, add eggs, coconut milk, fish sauce, garlic, salt and black pepper and beat until well combined.
2. Place the oil in the Instant Pot and select "Sauté" to heat the oil.
3. Select the "Cancel" and place the egg mixture.
4. Secure the lid and turn to "Seal" position.
5. Select "Steam" and just use the default time of 5 minutes.
6. Meanwhile, in a bowl, add the remaining ingredients and mix well.
7. Press the "Cancel" and allow a "Quick" release.

8. Carefully remove the lid and transfer the omelet onto a plate.
9. Place the chicken mixture over one half of omelet and fold it.
10. Serve immediately.

Nutrition Information

- Calories: 204
- Fat: 14.9g
- Saturated Fat: 5.4g
- Cholesterol: 285mg
- Sodium: 323mg
- Carbohydrates: 3.4g
- Fiber: 0.9g
- Sugar: 1.1g
- Protein: 15.3g

Soup & Stew Recipes

Chicken & Noodles Soup

Servings: 4

Prep Time: 40 minutes

Ingredients:

For Broth:

- 2 tablespoons canola oil
- 2 medium yellow onions, halved
- 1 (2-inch) piece fresh ginger, cut into ¼-inch slices
- 1 tablespoon coriander seeds
- 5 whole cloves
- 3 cardamom pods, lightly smashed
- 3 star anise pods
- 1 cinnamon stick
- 6 (5-ounce) bone-in, skin-on chicken thighs
- 3 tablespoons fish sauce
- 1 tablespoon sugar
- 8 cups water
- Salt and ground black pepper, as required

For Serving:

- 8 ounces rice noodles, prepared according to package's directions
- 3 scallions, sliced
- ½ cup bean sprouts

- ½ cup mixed fresh herbs (mint, cilantro and basil), chopped
- 1 lime, cut into wedges

Directions:

1. Add the oil in the Instant Pot and select "Sauté". Now, add the onions, cut side down, with the ginger and cook for about 4 minutes, without moving.
2. Stir in the whole spices and cook for about 1 minute.
3. Select the "Cancel" and stir in the chicken, fish sauce, sugar and water.
4. Secure the lid and turn to "Seal" position.
5. Cook on "Manual" with "High Pressure" for about 15 minutes.
6. Press the "Cancel" and allow a "Natural" release for about 10 minutes and then, allow a "Quick" release.
7. Carefully remove the lid and place the chicken thighs onto a plate.
8. Through a fine mesh strainer, strain the broth and season with the salt and black pepper.
9. Remove the bones from the chicken and then chop the meat.
10. Divide the cooked noodles and chopped into 4 serving bowls and top with the hot broth.
11. Serve with the topping of the scallions, bean sprouts and herbs.

Nutrition Information

- Calories: 593
- Fat: 23.3g
- Saturated Fat: 4.9g
- Cholesterol: 189mg
- Sodium: 1257mg
- Carbohydrates: 28.5g
- Fiber: 4.1g
- Sugar: 6.3g
- Protein: 65.3g

BEEF & NOODLES SOUP

Servings: 8

Prep Time: 1 hour 35 minutes

Ingredients:

For Broth:

- 1 tablespoon vegetable oil
- 4 pounds beef shanks
- 1 large onion, sliced thinly
- 1 tablespoon fresh ginger, sliced thinly
- 10½ cups water, divided
- ¼ cup fish sauce
- 2 tablespoons soy sauce
- 1 tablespoon sugar
- 2 star anise pods
- 1 cinnamon stick
- 4 whole cloves
- 1 teaspoon whole black peppercorns
- Salt, as required
- 1½ pounds beef brisket
- 10 cups of water

For Bowls:

- 1 pound thin rice noodles, prepared according to package's directions
- 2 cups bean sprouts
- 1 cup fresh cilantro leaves
- ½ cup fresh basil leaves
- 2-3 Serrano chilies, sliced thinly
- 2 tablespoons soy sauce

Directions:

1. Add the oil in the Instant Pot and select "Sauté". Now, add the beef shanks and sear for about 3 minutes per side.
2. With a slotted spoon, transfer the shanks into a bowl
3. In the pot, add the onions and ginger and cook for about 5-6 minutes.
4. Add ½ cup of water and scrape the browned bits from the bottom.
5. Select the "Cancel" and stir in the cooked beef shanks, fish sauce, soy sauce, sugar, whole spices and salt.
6. Arrange the beef brisket on top and place the remaining water.
7. Secure the lid and turn to "Seal" position.
8. Cook on "Manual" with "High Pressure" for about 60 minutes.
9. Press the "Cancel" and allow a "Natural" release.
10. Carefully remove the lid and transfer the shanks and brisket onto a plate.
11. Through a fine mesh strainer, strain the broth.
12. Remove the bones from the shanks and shred it.
13. Cut the brisket into thin slices against the grain crosswise.
14. Divide the cooked noodles and meat into 8 serving bowls and top with the hot broth.
15. Top each bowl with bean sprouts, herbs and Serrano chilies.
16. Drizzle with the soy sauce and serve.

Nutrition Information

- Calories: 728
- Fat: 21.8g
- Saturated Fat: 7.6g
- Cholesterol: 253mg
- Sodium: 1391mg
- Carbohydrates: 20.8g
- Fiber: 1.2g
- Sugar: 2.8g
- Protein: 106g

SHRIMP & CRAB SOUP

Servings: 6

Prep Time: 1 hour

Ingredients:

- 2 pounds pork ribs
- 4 tablespoons vegetable oil, divided
- 3 large shallots, halved
- 1 carrot, peeled and chopped roughly
- 5 teaspoons granulated sugar, divided
- Salt, as required
- 2 tablespoons fish sauce, divided
- 11 cups water, divided
- 1 cup cornstarch
- 2 pounds raw shrimp, peeled and deveined
- 1 shallot, chopped
- 5 garlic cloves, minced
- 1 pound lump crabmeat
- 10 ounces Udon noodles, prepared according to package's directions

For Topping:

- 3 scallions, chopped
- ½ cup fresh mint leaves, chopped
- 1 lime, cut into wedges

Directions:

1. In a pan of the boiling water, add the pork ribs and cook for about 4 minutes.
2. Drain the pork ribs and rinse well.
3. Place 1 tablespoon of the oil in the Instant Pot and select "Sauté". Now, add the halved 3 shallots and cook for about 2-3 minutes.
4. Select the "Cancel" and stir in the pork ribs, carrot, 4 teaspoons of sugar, salt, 1 tablespoon of fish sauce and 10 cups of water.
5. Secure the lid and turn to "Seal" position.
6. Cook on "Manual" with "High Pressure" for about 25 minutes.
7. Meanwhile, in a bowl, add the shrimp, 1 teaspoon of sugar, salt and remaining fish sauce and mix well.
8. Set aside for about 10 minutes.
9. Heat 3 tablespoons of oil in a large pan over medium heat and sauté the chopped shallot for about 3 minutes.
10. Stir in the garlic and sauté for about 1 minute.
11. Add the marinated shrimp and cook for about 2-3 minutes.
12. With tongs, transfer the shrimp into a bowl.
13. In the same skillet, add the crabmeat and toss with shallot mixture.
14. Remove from the heat and set aside.
15. Press the "Cancel" and allow a "Natural" release for about 15 minutes and then, allow a "Quick" release.
16. Meanwhile, in a bowl, add the cornstarch and remaining water and mix well.
17. Carefully remove the lid and through a fine mesh strainer, strain the broth.
18. Return the broth into the Instant Pot and select "Sauté".
19. Add the cornstarch mixture, stirring continuously and cook for about 2-3 minutes.
20. Divide the cooked noodles, shrimp and crabmeat into 6 serving bowls and top with the hot broth.
21. Top each bowl with scallion, mint and lime wedges and serve.

Nutrition Information

- Calories: 732
- Fat: 27.9g
- Saturated Fat: 5.9g
- Cholesterol: 391mg
- Sodium: 2000mg
- Carbohydrates: 63.8g
- Fiber: 3.9g
- Sugar: 8.6g
- Protein: 67.1g

BEEF STEW

Servings: 4

Prep Time: 35 minutes

Ingredients:

- 1 turnip, peeled and cut into chunks
- 2 carrots, peeled and cut into chunks
- ¼ cup beef broth
- 1 pound beef chuck stew meat
- 1 onion
- 1 tablespoon fresh ginger, minced
- 1 tablespoon garlic, minced
- 2 tablespoons tomato paste
- 1 tablespoon lemongrass paste
- 2 whole star anise
- 1 teaspoon curry powder
- Salt and ground black pepper, as required
- 2 tablespoons fish sauce
- 1½ cups water
- ½ cup coconut water
- ½ cup fresh cilantro, chopped

Directions:

1. In a small, heatproof container, place the carrots, turnip and broth. Set aside.
2. In the pot of Instant Pot, place the remaining ingredients except the cilantro and stir to combine.
3. Arrange a steamer trivet on top of beef mixture.

4. Place the container of vegetables on top of the trivet.
5. Secure the lid and turn to "Seal" position.
6. Cook on "Manual" with "High Pressure" for about 15 minutes.
7. Press the "Cancel" and allow a "Natural" release for about 10 minutes and then, allow a "Quick" release.
8. Carefully remove the lid and place the vegetable mixture into the stew.
9. Serve hot with the garnishing of cilantro.

Nutrition Information

- Calories: 305
- Fat: 15.6g
- Saturated Fat: 6.2g
- Cholesterol: 81mg
- Sodium: 940mg
- Carbohydrates: 12.8g
- Fiber: 3g
- Sugar: 6.3g
- Protein: 27.8g

PORK STEW

Servings: 8

Prep Time: 1 hour 10 minutes

Ingredients:

- 1 tablespoon coconut oil
- ¼ pound shiitake mushrooms, stems removed and halved
- ¼ cup shallots, sliced thinly
- 4 garlic cloves, smashed
- 1 tablespoon fresh ginger, sliced
- 3 pounds pork shoulder, cubed into 2-inch size
- 3 tablespoons fish sauce
- 1 cup coconut water
- 3 carrots, peeled and cut into ½-inch slices diagonally
- ½ cup fresh cilantro, chopped

Directions:

1. Add the oil in the Instant Pot and select "Sauté". Now, add the mushrooms and shallots and cook for about 3-5 minutes.
2. Stir in the garlic and ginger and cook for about 1 minute.
3. Add the pork cubes and cook for about 1-2 minutes.
4. Select the "Cancel" and stir in the fish sauce and coconut water.
5. Secure the lid and turn to "Seal" position.

6. Cook on "Manual" with "High Pressure" for about 40 minutes.
7. Press the "Cancel" and allow a "Natural" release for about 15 minutes and then, allow a "Quick" release.
8. Carefully remove the lid and with a spoon, transfer the pork cubes into a bowl.
9. In the pot, add the carrots and stir to combine.
10. Secure the lid and turn to "Seal" position.
11. Cook on "Manual" with "High Pressure" for about 2 minutes.
12. Press the "Cancel" and allow a "Natural" release for about 10 minutes and then, allow a "Quick" release.
13. Carefully remove the lid and mix in the pork cubes.
14. Serve hot with the garnishing of cilantro.

Nutrition Information

- Calories: 547
- Fat: 38.2g
- Saturated Fat: 14.9g
- Cholesterol: 153mg
- Sodium: 722mg
- Carbohydrates: 7.8g
- Fiber: 1.4g
- Sugar: 2.9g
- Protein: 40.9g

Noodles Recipes

Garlicky Noodles

Servings: 4

Prep Time: 20 minutes

Ingredients:

- 1 cup chicken broth
- 1 cup water
- 6 garlic cloves, minced
- 2 tablespoons brown sugar
- 2 tablespoons soy sauce
- 1 tablespoon fish sauce
- 1 teaspoon sesame oil
- 1 teaspoon chili paste
- 8 ounces noodles, broken in half
- 2 scallions, chopped

Directions:

1. In the pot of Instant Pot, place all the ingredients except the noodles and scallion and beat until well combined.
2. Place the noodles evenly on top of mixture.
3. Secure the lid and turn to "Seal" position.
4. Cook on "Manual" with "High Pressure" for about 6 minutes.
5. Press the "Cancel" and allow a "Quick" release.
6. Carefully remove the lid and mix the noodles with mixture.

7. Serve with the garnishing of scallions.

Nutrition Information

- Calories: 134
- Fat: 2.9g
- Saturated Fat: 0.5g
- Cholesterol: 17mg
- Sodium: 1012mg
- Carbohydrates: 22.2g
- Fiber: 1g
- Sugar: 5.6g
- Protein: 5g

NOODLES WITH VEGETABLES

Servings: 4

Prep Time: 20 minutes

Ingredients:

- 3 tablespoons peanut butter
- 2½ tablespoons soy sauce
- 1½ tablespoons rice vinegar
- 1 tablespoon fish sauce
- 1½ tablespoons honey
- ½ tablespoon chili paste
- Salt, as required
- 2 tablespoons vegetable oil
- 1 teaspoon fresh ginger, minced
- 4 garlic cloves, minced
- 2 medium carrots, peeled and sliced thinly
- 1 medium red bell pepper, seeded and sliced thinly
- 2 scallions, chopped
- 8 ounces noodles, broken into half
- 1½ cups water
- 2 tablespoons fresh lime juice
- 2 tablespoons fresh cilantro, chopped

Directions:

1. For sauce: in a bowl, add the peanut butter, soy sauce, vinegar, fish sauce, honey, chili paste and sat and beat until well combined.
2. Add the oil in the Instant Pot and select "Sauté". Now, add the garlic and ginger and cook for about 1 minute.

3. Add in the carrots, bell pepper and scallion and cook for about 1-2 minutes.
4. Select the "Cancel" and stir in the sauce.
5. Place the spaghetti over vegetable mixture and pour water on top.
6. Gently, press the noodles under water.
7. Secure the lid and turn to "Seal" position.
8. Cook on "Manual" with "High Pressure" for about 4 minutes.
9. Press the "Cancel" and allow a "Quick" release.
10. Carefully remove the lid and mix in the lime juice.
11. Serve with the garnishing of cilantro.

Nutrition Information

- Calories: 281
- Fat: 14.5g
- Saturated Fat: 2.9g
- Cholesterol: 17mg
- Sodium: 1050mg
- Carbohydrates: 32g
- Fiber: 3g
- Sugar: 11.9g
- Protein: 7.5g

VERMICELLI NOODLES WITH VEGGIES

Servings: 4

Prep Time: 20 minutes

Ingredients:

- 1 tablespoon vegetable oil
- 1 onion, chopped finely
- ¾ cup carrot, peeled and julienned
- ¾ cup red bell peppers, seeded and julienned
- 2 red chilies, chopped
- 2 cups vermicelli noodles
- ¼ teaspoon ground turmeric
- Salt, as required
- 1 tablespoon fish sauce
- 1 tablespoon soy sauce
- 2¼ cups water
- 2 scallions, sliced

Directions:

1. Add the oil in the Instant Pot and select "Sauté". Now, add the onions and cook for about 2 minutes.
2. Add in the carrot, bell pepper and red chili and cook for about 2 minutes.
3. Select the "Cancel" and stir in the remaining ingredients except the scallions.

4. Secure the lid and turn to "Seal" position.
5. Cook on "Manual" with "High Pressure" for about 1 minute.
6. Press the "Cancel" and allow a "Quick" release.
7. Carefully remove the lid and mix in the scallions.
8. Serve hot.

Nutrition Information

- Calories: 198
- Fat: 3.5g
- Saturated Fat: 0.7g
- Cholesterol: 0mg
- Sodium: 629mg
- Carbohydrates: 34.9g
- Fiber: 3.1g
- Sugar: 3.8g
- Protein: 6.1g

HONEY NOODLES WITH CHICKEN

Servings: 4

Prep Time: 20 minutes

Ingredients:

- 2 (6-ounce) skinless, boneless chicken breasts, chopped
- 3 tablespoons soy sauce
- 1 tablespoon fish sauce
- 1 tablespoon sesame oil
- 2 tablespoons honey
- ½ teaspoon chili paste
- 6 garlic cloves, minced
- 2 cups water
- 1 (8-ounce) package rice noodles
- 1 head broccoli, cut into small florets
- 1 yellow bell pepper, seeded and thinly sliced
- 1 orange bell pepper, seeded and thinly sliced
- 1 tablespoon sesame seeds

Directions:

1. In the pot of Instant Pot, place the chicken breasts, soy sauce, fish sauce, oil, honey, chili paste, garlic cloves and water and mix well.
2. Place the rice noodles on top and gently, press into the water.
3. Secure the lid and turn to "Seal" position.

4. Cook on "Manual" with "High Pressure" for about 2 minutes.
5. Press the "Cancel" and allow a "Quick" release.
6. Carefully remove the lid and immediately, stir in the broccoli and bell peppers.
7. Immediately, secure the lid for about 5-10 minutes.
8. Remove lid and serve with the garnishing of sesame seeds.

Nutrition Information

- Calories: 427
- Fat: 6.4g
- Saturated Fat: 0.7g
- Cholesterol: 49mg
- Sodium: 1216mg
- Carbohydrates: 67.5g
- Fiber: 3.7g
- Sugar: 13.2g
- Protein: 25.5g

NOODLES WITH SHRIMP

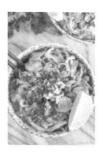

Servings: 4

Prep Time: 25 minutes

Ingredients:

- 8 ounces rice noodles
- 4 tablespoons vegetable oil, divided
- 1/3 cup brown sugar
- 3 tablespoons rice vinegar
- 3 tablespoons fish sauce
- 2 tablespoons soy sauce
- 4 scallions, chopped and divided
- 2 garlic cloves, chopped
- 2 carrots, peeled and cut into thin strips
- 1 cup red bell pepper, seeded and sliced into thin strips
- 1 cup yellow bell pepper, seeded and sliced into thin strips
- 3 large eggs, beaten
- 1 pound shrimp, peeled and deveined
- 1 tablespoon fresh lime juice

Directions:

1. In a large bowl of boiling water, soak the rice noodles for about 5 minutes.
2. Drain the noodles and mix 1 tablespoon of oil. Set aside.
3. For sauce: in another bowl, add the brown sugar, vinegar, soy sauce and fish sauce and beat until well combined.

4. Place the remaining oil in the Instant Pot and select "Sauté". Then add 2 scallions and garlic and cook for about 1 minute.
5. Stir in the bell peppers and carrots and cook for about 2 minutes.
6. Push the mixture to the edge of the pan.
7. In the center of pan, place the beaten eggs and cook for about 1-2 minutes, stirring continuously.
8. Add the bell peppers and cook for about 1 minute.
9. Select the "Cancel" and stir in the shrimp.
10. Secure the lid and turn to "Seal" position.
11. Cook on "Manual" with "High Pressure" for about 1 minute.
12. Press the "Cancel" and allow a "Natural" release for about 5 minutes and then, allow a "Quick" release.
13. Carefully remove the lid and mix in the noodles and sauce.
14. Immediately secure the lid for about 10 minutes.
15. Remove lid and stir in the lime juice.
16. Serve with the garnishing of remaining scallions.

Nutrition Information

- Calories: 472
- Fat: 19.6g
- Saturated Fat: 4.4g
- Cholesterol: 378mg
- Sodium: 1800mg
- Carbohydrates: 38.2g
- Fiber: 2.6g
- Sugar: 17.5g
- Protein: 33.5g

VEGETABLES & VEGETARIAN RECIPES

STEWED SQUASH

Servings: 6

Prep Time: 20 minutes

Ingredients:

- 2 tablespoons vegetable oil
- 1 tablespoon garlic, chopped
- 1 (2½-pound) butternut squash, peeled and cut into 1-inch cubes
- 2 tablespoons fish sauce
- 1 tablespoon sugar
- Salt and ground black pepper, as required
- ¾ cup vegetable broth

Directions:

1. Add the oil in the Instant Pot and select "Sauté". Now, add the garlic and cook for about 1 minute.
2. Add the squash cues and cook for about 1 minute.
3. Select the "Cancel" and stir in the remaining ingredients.
4. Secure the lid and turn to "Seal" position.
5. Cook on "Manual" with "High Pressure" for about 4 minutes.
6. Press the "Cancel" and allow a "Natural" release.
7. Carefully remove the lid and serve hot.

Nutrition Information

- Calories: 142
- Fat: 4.9g
- Saturated Fat: 1g
- Cholesterol: 0mg
- Sodium: 954mg
- Carbohydrates: 24.9g
- Fiber: 3.8g
- Sugar: 6.5g
- Protein: 2.9g

VEGETARIAN CURRY

Servings: 4

Prep Time: 25 minutes

Ingredients:

- 2 tablespoons canola oil
- 3 tablespoons curry paste
- 1 (19-ounce) can coconut milk
- 14 ounces firm tofu, pressed and cubed
- 1 carrot, peeled and sliced
- 1 red bell pepper, seeded and chopped into 1-inch pieces
- 1 green bell pepper, seeded and chopped into 1-inch pieces
- 2 scallions, cut into 2-inch pieces
- 1 teaspoon fresh ginger, grated
- 1 tablespoon fresh lime juice
- 1 tablespoon fish sauce
- 1 teaspoon sugar

Directions:

1. Add the oil in the Instant Pot and select "Sauté". Now, add the curry paste and sauté for about 30 seconds.
2. Add the coconut milk and stir well.
3. Select the "Cancel" and stir in tofu, carrot, bell peppers, scallion and ginger.
4. Secure the lid and turn to "Seal" position.
5. Cook on "Manual" with "Low Pressure" for about 2 minutes.

6. Press the "Cancel" and allow a "Quick" release.
7. Carefully remove the lid and mix in the remaining ingredients.
8. Serve hot.

Nutrition Information

- Calories: 551
- Fat: 50g
- Saturated Fat: 29.9g
- Cholesterol: 0mg
- Sodium: 393mg
- Carbohydrates: 20.4g
- Fiber: 5.3g
- Sugar: 10.2g
- Protein: 12.9g

Tofu & Green Beans Curry

Servings: 5

Prep Time: 35 minutes

Ingredients:

For Green Beans:

- 1 pound fresh green beans, trimmed and chopped into 1½-inch pieces
- 1 cup water

For Curry:

- 1 (14-ounce) can coconut milk
- ½ cup water
- 3 tablespoons peanut butter
- 2 tablespoons plus 1 teaspoon curry paste
- 1 tablespoon coconut oil
- 2 dried red chilies, broken into pieces
- 1 small onion, chopped
- ¼ cup raw cashews
- 2 teaspoons fresh ginger, grated
- 2 teaspoons garlic, grated
- 3 teaspoons rice vinegar
- 1 teaspoon fish sauce
- 1 teaspoon soy sauce
- 1 teaspoon coconut sugar
- ¼ teaspoon ground turmeric
- 8 ounces extra-firm tofu, drained and cubed
- 1 tablespoon fresh lime juice

Directions:

1. For green beans: In the bottom of Instant Pot, arrange a steamer trivet and pour water.
2. Place green beans on top of the trivet.
3. Secure the lid and turn to "Seal" position.
4. Cook on "Manual" with "High Pressure" for about 5 minutes.
5. Press the "Cancel" and allow a "Quick" release.
6. Carefully, remove the lid and transfer the green beans into a bowl. Set aside.
7. Remove the water from the pot and with paper towels, pat dry it.
8. For curry: in a bowl, add the coconut milk, water, peanut butter, water and curry paste and beat until well combined. Keep aside.
9. Add the oil in the Instant Pot and select "Sauté". Now, add the dried red chili and cook for about 30 seconds.
10. Add the onion and cook for about 1 minute.
11. Add cashews and cook for about 1 minute.
12. Stir in the ginger and garlic and cook for about 1 minute.
13. Add the coconut milk mixture and cook for about 1 minute.
14. Select the "Cancel" and stir in remaining ingredients except the lime juice.
15. Secure the lid and turn to "Seal" position.
16. Cook on "Manual" with "High Pressure" for about 2 minutes.
17. Press the "Cancel" and allow a "Quick" release.
18. Carefully remove the lid and select "Sauté".
19. Stir in green beans and cook for about 1-2 minutes.
20. Select the "Cancel" and stir in lime juice before serving.

Nutrition Information

- Calories: 428
- Fat: 36g
- Saturated Fat: 21.1g
- Cholesterol: 0mg

- Sodium: 220mg
- Carbohydrates: 20.8g
- Fiber: 6.2g
- Sugar: 6.9g
- Protein: 12.1g

CARAMELIZED TOFU

Servings: 4

Prep Time: 25 minutes

Ingredients:

- ¾ cup water
- 2 tablespoons cornstarch
- 2 tablespoons granulated sugar
- 1 teaspoon fresh ginger, minced
- 2 garlic cloves, minced
- ¼ cup soy sauce
- 3 tablespoons rice wine vinegar
- ½ teaspoon red pepper flakes, crushed
- 2 tablespoons vegetable oil
- 16 ounces extra-firm tofu, pressed and cut into ½-inch thick pieces.

Directions:

1. In a bowl, add all the ingredients except the tofu and oil and beat until well combined.
2. Add the oil in the Instant Pot and select "Sauté". Now, add the tofu and cook for about 2-3 minutes or until browned from all sides.
3. Select the "Cancel" and stir in the sauce.
4. Secure the lid and turn to "Seal" position.
5. Cook on "Manual" with "High Pressure" for about 5 minutes.
6. Press the "Cancel" and allow a "Quick" release.
7. Carefully remove the lid and serve.

Nutrition Information

- Calories: 222
- Fat: 13.5g
- Saturated Fat: 2g
- Cholesterol: 0mg
- Sodium: 910mg
- Carbohydrates: 14.1g
- Fiber: 0.8g
- Sugar: 6.9g
- Protein: 12.4g

STEAMED SPRING ROLLS

Servings: 10

Prep Time: 25 minutes

Ingredients:

- 5 ounces dried rice vermicelli, soaked for 10 minutes and drained
- 1 cup carrot, peeled and grated
- ½ cup fresh bean sprouts
- 3 tablespoons fresh cilantro leaves, chopped
- 2 tablespoons soy sauce
- 1 tablespoons fresh lime juice
- 1 tablespoon chili jam
- 1½ tablespoons granulated sugar
- 1 tablespoon fried garlic
- 10 (10-inch) dried rice paper wrappers
- 2 cups water

Directions:

1. For the filling: place all the ingredients except the wrappers and water in a large bowl and mix well.
2. Fill a shallow bowl with warm water.
3. Dip 1 rice wrapper into the water until it is pliable.
4. Now, arrange the wrapper on a smooth surface.
5. Place about 1-2 tablespoons of filling in the center of the rice paper.
6. Carefully fold the wrapper around the filling.
7. Repeat with the remaining wrappers and filling.
8. In the bottom of Instant Pot, arrange the steamer basket and pour the water.

9. Place the rolls in steamer basket.
10. Secure the lid and turn to "Seal" position.
11. Select "Steam" and just use the default time of 3 minutes.
12. Press the "Cancel" and allow a "Natural" release.
13. Carefully remove the lid and serve warm.

Nutrition Information

- Calories: 119
- Fat: 0.2g
- Saturated Fat: 0.1g
- Cholesterol: 0mg
- Sodium: 238mg
- Carbohydrates: 27.5g
- Fiber: 0.8g
- Sugar: 3.9g
- Protein: 1.5g

DESSERT RECIPES

SWEET SOUP

Servings: 5

Prep Time: 25 minutes

Ingredients:

- 1/3 cup tapioca strips, shredded
- 2 cups water
- 1 pound sweet potato, peeled cubed and soaked in salted water for 5 minutes
- ½-1 cup kelp strips, washed thoroughly, soaked in warm water for 5 minutes and rinsed
- ½ cup peeled split mung beans, rinsed
- 1 (13½-ounce) can coconut milk
- ½-¾ cup sugar
- ½ teaspoon vanilla extract
- 2 cups milk

Directions:

1. In the pot of Instant Pot, place the tapioca strips and water and stir to combine.
2. Secure the lid and turn to "Seal" position.
3. Cook on "Manual" with "High Pressure" for about 3 minutes.

4. Press the "Cancel" and allow a "Quick" release.
5. Carefully, remove the lid and mix in the sweet potato, seaweed strips, mung beans, coconut milk, sugar and vanilla extract.
6. Secure the lid and turn to "Seal" position.
7. Cook on "Manual" with "High Pressure" for about 5 minutes.
8. Press the "Cancel" and allow a "Natural" release for about 10 minutes and then, allow a "Quick" release.
9. Carefully remove the lid and select "Sauté".
10. Mix in the milk and bring to a gentle boil.
11. Select the "Cancel" and serve immediately.

Nutrition Information

- Calories: 487
- Fat: 20.6g
- Saturated Fat: 17.4g
- Cholesterol: 8mg
- Sodium: 132mg
- Carbohydrates: 70.4g
- Fiber: 9.5g
- Sugar: 43g
- Protein: 12.3g

RICE PUDDING

Servings: 6

Prep Time: 25 minutes

Ingredients:

- 3 cups whole milk
- ¾ cup jasmine rice, rinsed
- ½ cup granulated sugar
- 1 strip lime peel
- Pinch of salt
- 1 cup canned coconut milk
- 1 teaspoon vanilla extract
- 1/8 teaspoon ground cinnamon

Directions:

1. In the pot of Instant Pot, place the milk, rice, sugar, lime peel and salt and stir to combine.
2. Secure the lid and turn to "Seal" position.
3. Select "Porridge" and just use the default time of 15 minutes.
4. Press the "Cancel" and allow a "Natural" release for about 10 minutes and then, allow a "Quick" release.
5. Carefully remove the lid and discard the lime peel.
6. Stir in the coconut milk and vanilla extract.
7. Serve warm with the sprinkling of cinnamon.

Nutrition Information

- Calories: 310
- Fat: 13.5g

- Saturated Fat: 10.7g
- Cholesterol: 12mg
- Sodium: 82mg
- Carbohydrates: 42.5g
- Fiber: 1.9g
- Sugar: 24.5g
- Protein: 6.4g

Rice & Black-Eyed Peas Pudding

Servings: 6

Prep Time: 30 minutes

Ingredients:

For Pudding:

- 1 (15½-ounce) can black-eye peas, drained and rinsed thoroughly
- 1 cup sweet rice, rinsed and drained
- 1 cup sugar
- 1 teaspoon vanilla extract
- 4 cups water

For Coconut Sauce:

- 1 tablespoon cornstarch
- 2 tablespoons water
- 1 (14-ounce) can coconut milk
- ½ cup water
- 1 Pandan leaf
- 1 tablespoon sugar
- ½ teaspoon salt

Directions:

1. For the pudding: in the pot of Instant Pot, place all the ingredients and stir to combine.
2. Secure the lid and turn to "Seal" position.
3. Cook on "Manual" with "Low Pressure" for about 14 minutes.

4. Meanwhile, for coconut sauce: in a bowl, add the cornstarch and water and mix well.
5. In a pan, add the coconut milk, water, Pandan leaf, sugar and salt over medium heat and bring to a gentle boil.
6. Slowly, add the cornstarch mixture, stirring continuously.
7. Remove from the heat and set aside.
8. Press the "Cancel" and allow a "Quick" release.
9. Carefully remove the lid and quickly, put the pudding into a large serving bowl.
10. Add the coconut sauce and stir to combine.
11. Serve warm.

Nutrition Information

- Calories: 585
- Fat: 15.8g
- Saturated Fat: 14g
- Cholesterol: 0mg
- Sodium: 234mg
- Carbohydrates: 111.2g
- Fiber: 21.9g
- Sugar: 39g
- Protein: 21.3g

Coffee Flan

Servings: 7

Prep Time: 30 minutes

Ingredients:

- ¾ cup granulated sugar
- 1 cup plus 2 tablespoon water, divided
- 1 cup sweetened condensed milk
- 2 whole eggs
- 2 egg yolks
- 2 cups whole milk
- 2 tablespoons instant coffee powder
- 1 cup water

Directions:

1. In a pan, add the sugar and 2 tablespoon of the water over medium-low heat and cook until the sugar turns into a golden amber color.
2. Remove from the heat and immediately, place about 1½ tablespoons of the caramel into each of the 7 (4-ounce) ramekins.
3. Set aside to cool and harden.
4. In a large bowl, add the condensed milk, whole eggs and egg yolks and beat until smooth.
5. In a pan, add 1 cup of milk over medium heat and cook until it starts to bubble.
6. Remove from the heat and add the coffee powder, stirring continuously until dissolved.
7. Add the remaining milk and mix well.

8. Add the milk mixture into the bowl of egg mixture and mix until well combined.
9. Through a fine mesh sieve, strain the flan mixture.
10. Carefully place the mixture into the ramekins over caramel.
11. With 1 piece of the foil, cover each ramekin well.
12. In the bottom of Instant Pot, arrange the steamer trivet and pour the water.
13. Place the ramekins on top of the trivet.
14. Secure the lid and turn to "Seal" position.
15. Cook on "Manual" with "High Pressure" for about 6 minutes.
16. Press the "Cancel" and allow a "Natural" release for about 10 minutes and then, allow a "Quick" release.
17. Carefully remove the lid and place the ramekins onto a counter.
18. Carefully remove the foil and let them cool for about 60-90 minutes.
19. With 1 plastic wrap, cover each ramekin and refrigerate overnight.
20. Carefully place each flan onto a serving plate and serve.

Nutrition Information

- Calories: 296
- Fat: 8.6g
- Saturated Fat: 4.6g
- Cholesterol: 129mg
- Sodium: 103mg
- Carbohydrates: 48.6g
- Fiber: 0g
- Sugar: 49g
- Protein: 8.1g

Coconut Flan

Servings: 6

Prep Time: 25 minutes

Ingredients:

- 1 (13½-ounce) can coconut milk
- 14 ounces sweetened condensed milk
- 12 ounces evaporated milk
- 1 cup full-fat milk
- 3 eggs
- 1 cup sugar
- Pinch of salt
- ¼ teaspoon vanilla extract
- 2 cups water
- ½ cup desiccated coconut

Directions:

1. For caramel syrup: in a pan, add the sugar over medium heat and cook for 5 minutes or until it changes into a golden amber color, stirring frequently.
2. Remove from the heat and immediately, place the caramel syrup into a 6-inch aluminum cake tin evenly.
3. In a blender, add the remaining ingredients except the water and coconut and pulse until well combined.
4. Through a mesh strainer, strain the mixture into the cake tin over caramel syrup evenly.
5. With a piece of the foil, cover the cake tin.
6. In the bottom of Instant Pot, arrange the steamer trivet and pour the water.
7. Arrange the cake tin on top of the trivet.

8. Secure the lid and turn to "Seal" position.
9. Cook on "Manual" with "High Pressure" for about 15 minutes.
10. Press the "Cancel" and allow a "Natural" release.
11. Carefully remove the lid and transfer the cake tin onto a counter.
12. Carefully remove the foil and let it cool completely.
13. With 1 plastic wrap, cover the tin and refrigerate overnight.
14. Carefully place the flan onto a serving plate and sprinkle with coconut.
15. Cut into desired sized pieces and serve.

Nutrition Information

- Calories: 636
- Fat: 30.5g
- Saturated Fat: 22.9g
- Cholesterol: 124mg
- Sodium: 235mg
- Carbohydrates: 81.7g
- Fiber: 2g
- Sugar: 79.6g
- Protein: 14.9g

CONCLUSION

Vietnamese cuisine is very rich in aromas, taste and is very healthy despite the fact that the landscape of the country is very versatile, the Vietnamese cuisine is rich in lemongrass, cilantro, simmered beef bones, mint and least to forget, the fish sauces. The food always has a balanced proportion of sweetness, fish-sauciness, aromatics, sourness, and heat. The basic theme of the cuisine is based on the 'yin and yang' principles, i.e. warm and cool, salty and sweet, and fermented and fresh. Just like the Chinese cuisine, the Vietnamese cuisine is based on the five flavor elements i.e. bitter, sweet, salty, sour, and spicy.

Made in the USA
San Bernardino, CA
03 December 2019

60776435R00069